ng a
Jelly

oems

hn Foster

OXFORD
UNIVERSITY PRESS

OXFORD
UNIVERSITY PRESS

Great Clarendon Street, Oxford OX2 6DP

Oxford University Press is a department of the University of Oxford.
It furthers the University's objective of excellence in research, scholarship,
and education by publishing worldwide in

Oxford New York

Athens Auckland Bangkok Bogotá Buenos Aires
Cape Town Chennai Dar es Salaam Delhi Florence Hong Kong Istanbul
Karachi Kolkata Kuala Lumpur Madrid Melbourne Mexico City Mumbai
Nairobi Paris São Paulo Shanghai Singapore Taipei Tokyo Toronto
Warsaw

with associated companies in Berlin Ibadan

Oxford is a registered trade mark of Oxford University Press
in the UK and in certain other countries

British Library Cataloguing in Publication Data available

ISBN 0 19 2762850

10 9 8 7 6 5 4 3 2 1

Printed in China

We are grateful to the authors for permission to reprint the following poems.

First published in John Foster (ed.): *Little Miss Dimble* (OUP, 2000):
Tara Grant: 'Riddle-Me-Ree, One, Two, Three', © Tara Grant 2000; **Tony
Langham:** 'Scream Cream', © Tony Langham 2000; **Michaela Morgan:**
'Rabbit', © Michaela Morgan 2000; **Brian Moses:** 'The Aquarium', © Brian
Moses 2000; **Claire Pepperell:** 'Snail', © Claire Pepperell 2000; **John Rice:**
'Metal Fettle', © John Rice 2000.

First published in John Foster (ed.): *I'm Not Scared of the Monster* (OUP, 2000):
Robin Mellor: 'Recipe for a Dragon', © Robin Mellor 2000; **Irene Rawnsley:**
'Dog's Dinner', © Irene Rawnsley 2000; **Cynthia Rider:** 'Hurry, Scurry', ©
Cynthia Rider 2000.

We are also grateful for permission to reprint the following poems:

John Agard: 'No Hickory No Dickory No Dock' from *No Hickory, No Dickory,
No Dock* (Viking Kestrel, 1991), reprinted by permission of Caroline Sheldon
Literary Agency on behalf of the author; **Charles Causley:** 'Charity Chadder'
from *Early in the Morning* (Puffin), reprinted by permission of David Higham
Associates; **June Crebbin:** 'Kite' from *The Jungle Sale* (Viking Kestrel, 1988), ©
June Crebbin 1988, reprinted by permission of the author; **John Cotton:**
'Pineapple', © John Cotton 1998, first published in John Foster (ed.): *Word
Whirls* (OUP 1998), reprinted by permission of the author; **Michael Dugan:**
'Herbaceous Plodd' from *My Old Dad and Other Funny Things Like Him*
(Cheshire/Ginn, Melbourne, 1976), © Michael Dugan 1976, reprinted by
permission of the author; **Richard Edwards:** 'Humpty Dumpty' from
Nonsense Nursery Rhymes (OUP), reprinted by permission of the author; **John
Foster:** 'I'm Not Scared of the Monster' from *Bare Bear and Other Rhymes*,
(OUP, 1999), © John Foster 1999, reprinted by permission of the author;
Marilyn Helmer: 'Jack's the Finest Flapjack Flipper' first published in *SPIDER*
magazine, April 1998, Vol 5, No 4, © 1998 by Marilyn Helmer, by
permission of *SPIDER* magazine, Cricket Magazine Group; **Dennis Lee:** 'Little
Miss Dimble' from *Garbage Delight* (Macmillan of Canada, 1977), © 1977
Dennis Lee, reprinted by permission of the author, c/o Westwood Creative
Artists; **Spike Milligan:** 'On the Ning Nang Nong' from *Silly Verse for Kids*
(Puffin, 1968), reprinted by permission of Spike Milligan Productions Ltd;
Michael Rosen: 'Jack and Jill' from *Michael Rosen's ABC* (Macdonald Young
Books, 1995), © Michael Rosen 1995, reprinted by permission of PFD on
behalf of the author; **David Whitehead:** 'Leopard', © David Whitehead
1996, first published in John Foster (ed.): *Crack Another Yolk* (OUP, 1996),
reprinted by permission of the author.

Despite efforts to obtain permission from all copyright holders before
publication, this has not been possible in a few cases. If notified the
publisher will be pleased to rectify any errors or omissions at the earliest
opportunity.

The illustrations are by:
Diana Catchpole p. 8; Louise Comfort pp. 28–29; Steve Cox pp. 14–15, 32;
Dorian Davies pp. 10–11, 20–21;
Peet Ellison pp. 24–25; Jan McCafferty pp. 22–23; Kaoru Miyake pp. 9, 12-13;
Sara Silcock pp. 18–19, 26;
Claire Tindall pp. 4–5, 27; Gillian Tofts pp. 6–7; Stephen Waterhouse pp.
16–17, 30-31

List of contents:

Recipe for a Dragon	Robin Mellor	4
The Aquarium	Brian Moses	6
Leopard	David Whitehead	8
Hippopotamus	Michael Flanders	8
Charity Chadder	Charles Causley	9
Riddle-Me-Ree, One, Two, Three	Tara Grant	10
Riddle	Traditional	11
Pineapple	John Cotton	11
Dog's Dinner	Irene Rawnsley	12
Betty Botter	Traditional	14
Jack's the Finest Flapjack Flipper	Marilyn Helmer	15
On the Ning Nang Nong	Spike Milligan	16
Jack and Jill	Michael Rosen	18
Humpty Dumpty	Richard Edwards	18
Little Miss Dimble	Dennis Lee	19
Twinkle, Twinkle Little Bat!	Lewis Carroll	19
Metal Fettle	John Rice	20
Kite	June Crebbin	21
Snail	Claire Pepperell	21
Scream Cream	Tony Langham	22
Hurry, Scurry	Cynthia Rider	24
The Goblin	Jack Prelutsky	25
Rabbit	Michaela Morgan	26
Herbaceous Plodd	Michael Dugan	27
I'm Not Scared of the Monster	John Foster	28
The Jumblies	Edward Lear	30
No Hickory No Dickory No Dock	John Agard	32

Recipe for a Dragon

Take hot chilli peppers
numbering three,
add four cups of sulphur
and the sting of a bee.

Rub two sticks together
to make smoke and spark.
Borrow breath from a glow worm
who lights up the dark.

From a Winter bonfire
lift the heart of an ember
to put with some leaves
from fiery September.

Place all the ingredients
in an old metal pot,
ignite with a sunbeam
and stir up the lot.

Just when you're thinking
that nothing will happen,
out of the white steam
will come a small dragon.

Robin Mellor

The Aquarium

The aquarium
was disappointing.

The dogfish
didn't bark,
the jellyfish
didn't wobble.

The sea mouse
didn't squeak,
the starfish
didn't shine.

squeak
squeak!

The hermit crabs
were crabby,
the clams
clammed up,
and the plaice
stayed in one place.

But when the swordfish
attacked us,
and the sharks invited us
to be their lunch...

we rode away fast...
on a sea horse!

Brian Moses

Leopard

The leopard is a crafty cat
His camouflage is dotted
He hides among the dappled leaves
Yet, even then he's spotted.

David Whitehead

Hippopotamus

What fun   to be
A Hippo   -potamus
And weigh   a ton
From top   to bottamus.

Michael Flanders

Charity Chadder

Charity Chadder
Borrowed a ladder,
Leaned it against the moon,
Climbed to the top
Without a stop
On the 31st of June,
Brought down every single star,
Kept them all in a pickle jar.

Charles Causley

Riddle-Me-Ree, One, Two, Three

When there's nothing in me,
I'm thin and quite small,
When you fill me with air
I'm round as a ball.
When you let the air out,
I whizz round and round
And as I am flying
I make a rude sound.

Tara Grant

Riddle

Thirty white horses on a red hill,
    First they champ,
    Then they stamp,
Then they stand still.

Traditional

Pineapple

My face is quite rough and quite scaly,
And my hair's a bit like a punk's,
But inside I'm sweet and a bit of a treat,
With ice-cream and cut up in chunks.

John Cotton

Dog's Dinner

On Thursday night
my mother said
that I could sleep
in the barleysugar bed.

I dreamed of sailing
a bubble gum boat
blown big as a dinosaur
to keep me afloat.

On Friday night
my mother said
my sister could sleep
in the barleysugar bed.

She dreamed of
a liquorice homework book
that ate the sums
when she was stuck.

On Saturday
my mother said
she would like to sleep
in the barleysugar bed.

She dreamed
of a trifle covered in cream
with lollipop spoons
to lick it clean.

When Sunday came
my mother said
the dog could sleep
on the barleysugar bed.

He ate it.

Irene Rawnsley

Betty Botter

Betty Botter bought some butter,
"But," she said, "the butter's bitter;
If I put it in my batter
It will make my batter bitter,
But a bit of better butter
Will make my batter better."
So she bought a bit of butter
Better than her bitter butter,
And the batter was not bitter.
So 'twas better Betty Botter
Bought a bit of better butter.

Traditional

Jack's the Finest Flapjack Flipper

Jack's the finest flapjack flipper.
No one flips a flapjack finer
than the flapjacks Jack flips finely
at Jack's Finest Flapjack Diner.

Marilyn Helmer

On the Ning Nang Nong

On the Ning Nang Nong
Where the cows go Bong!
And the monkeys all say Boo!
There's a Nong Nang Ning
Where the trees go Ping!
And the tea-pots Jibber Jabber Joo!
On the Ning Nang Nong
All the mice go Clong!
And you just can't catch 'em when they do!
So it's Ning Nang Nong!
Cows go Bong!
Nong Nang Ning
Trees go Ping!
Nong Ning Nang
The mice go Clang!
What a noisy place to belong
Is the Ning Nang Ning Nang Nong!

Spike Milligan

Jack and Jill

Jack and Jill went up the hill
Juggling a jug of jelly.
A passing bug jumped in the jug
which made the jelly smelly.

Michael Rosen

Humpty Dumpty

Humpty Dumpty sat on a wall,
Humpty Dumpty had a great fall.
He didn't get bruised, he didn't get bumped,
Humpty Dumpty bungee-jumped.

Richard Edwards

Little Miss Dimble

Little Miss Dimble
Lived in a thimble,
Slept in a measuring spoon.
She met a mosquito,
And called him 'My sweet-o',
And married him under the moon.

Dennis Lee

Twinkle, Twinkle Little Bat!

Twinkle, twinkle little bat!
How I wonder what you're at!
Up above the world you fly,
Like a tea-tray in the sky.

Lewis Carroll

Metal Fettle

The clank of a tank,
the chink of chains,
the tinkle of tins,
the rattle of trains.

The click of a clasp,
the clang of a bell,
the creak of a hinge,
the chime of a spell.

The shatter of cymbals,
the clash of swords,
the clatter of cutlery,
the twang of chords.

The ping of keys,
the song of a wheel,
the plink of pans,
the ring of steel.

John Rice

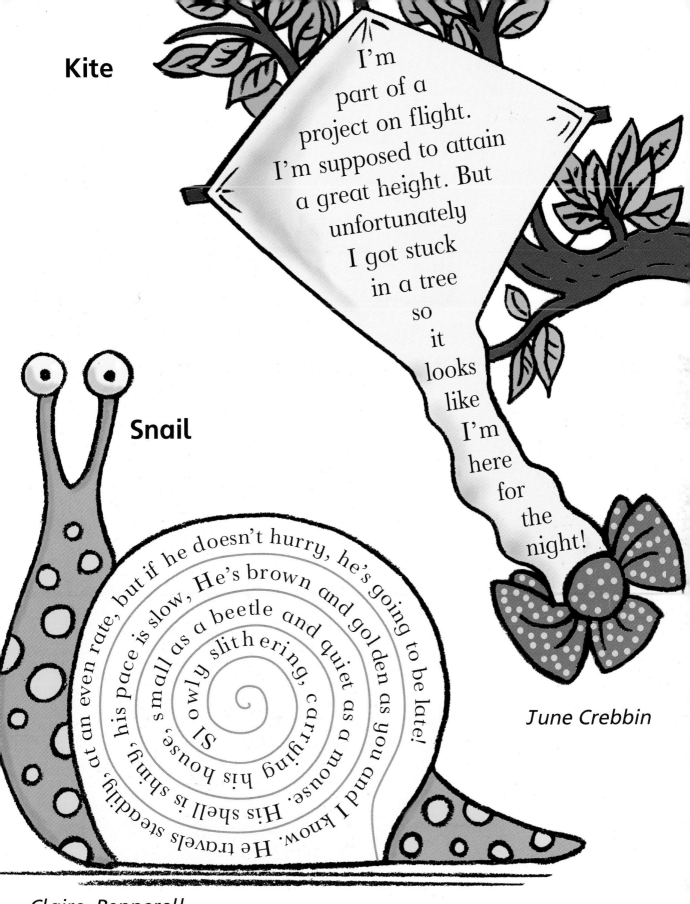

Kite

I'm part of a project on flight. I'm supposed to attain a great height. But unfortunately I got stuck in a tree so it looks like I'm here for the night!

June Crebbin

Snail

at an even rate, but if he doesn't hurry, he's going to be late! He's brown and golden as you and I know, small as a beetle and quiet as a mouse. His shell is shiny, his pace is slow, He travels steadily, carrying his house, SI owly slithering

Claire Pepperell

21

Scream Cream

I scream
you scream
'cos there
are mice
in our
ice-cream.

Mice
in our
ice-cream
should call
it mice-cream.

Mice
in our
ice-cream
not very
nice cream.

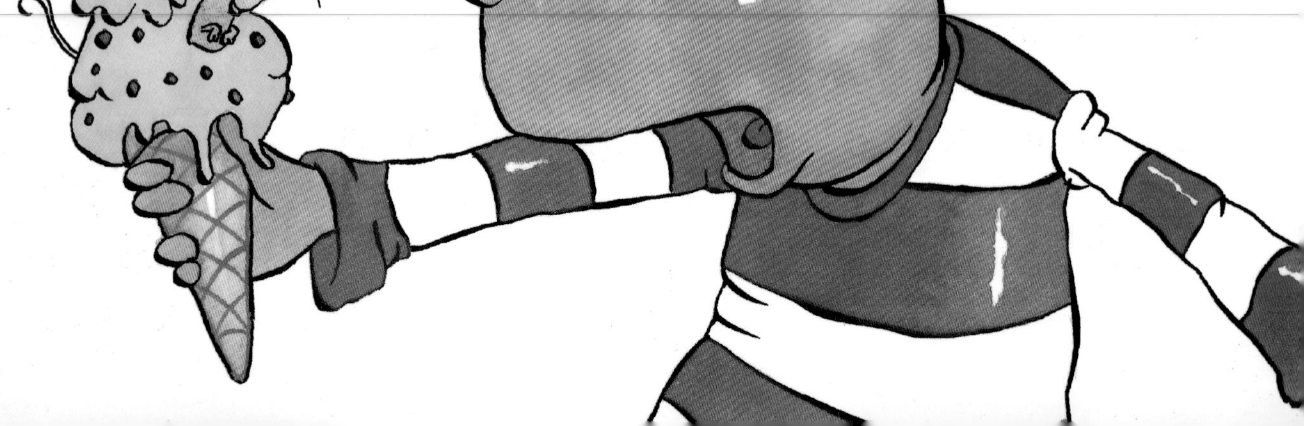

Mice
in our
ice-cream
sounds like
a bad dream.

So I scream
and you scream
together
we're a
scream team –

aaaaaaaaaarrrrrrrrgggggggggghhhhhhhh!

Tony Langham

Hurry, Scurry

Hurry, scurry,
Run inside.
Hurry, scurry,
Run and hide.
Don't try to pry.
Don't try to spy.
The goblin folk
Are passing by.
Lock your doors
And curl up tight.
The mischievous goblins
Are out tonight!

Cynthia Rider

The Goblin

There's a goblin as green
As a goblin can be
Who is sitting outside
And is waiting for me.

When he knocked on my door
And said softly, "Come play."
I answered, "No thank you,
Now, please, go away."

But the goblin as green
As a goblin can be
Is still sitting outside
And is waiting for me.

Jack Prelutsky

Rabbit

Thumb licker
bowl kicker
nose twitcher
scratch scritcher
carrot cruncher
lettuce muncher
straw robber
tailbobber
rabbit

Michaela Morgan

Herbaceous Plodd

Herbaceous Plodd
is rather odd.
His eyes are red,
his nose is blue,
his neck and head
are joined by glue.
He only dines
on unripe peas,
bacon rinds
and melted cheese.
He rarely talks,
he never smiles,
but goes for walks
with crocodiles.

Michael Dugan

I'm Not Scared of the Monster

I'm not scared of the monster
That hides beneath my bed.
When it leaps out
To prowl about,
I pat it on the head.

I'm not scared of the monster
That lurks behind the door.
When it leaps out
To prowl about
I shake its furry paw.

I'm not scared of the monster
That skulks under the chair.
When it leaps out
To prowl about
I stroke its spiky hair.

I'm not scared of the monsters,
'Cause they're no longer there.
When I leapt out
To scream and shout,
I gave them all a scare!

John Foster

The Jumblies

They went to sea in a Sieve, they did,
    In a Sieve they went to sea;
In spite of all their friends could say,
On a winter's morn, on a stormy day,
    In a Sieve they went to sea!
And when the Sieve turned round and round,
And everyone cried, "You'll all be drowned!"
They called aloud, "Our Sieve ain't big,
But we don't care a button, we don't care a fig!
    In a Sieve we'll go to sea."
       Far and few, far and few,
          Are the lands where the Jumblies live;
        Their heads are green, and their hands are blue,
          And they went to sea in a Sieve.

from The Jumblies by Edward Lear

No Hickory No Dickory No Dock

Wasn't me
Wasn't me
said the little mouse
I didn't run up no clock

You could hickory me
You could dickory me
or lock me in a dock

I still say
I didn't run up no clock

Was me who run under your bed
Was me who bit into your bread
Was me who nibbled your cheese

But please please
I didn't run up no clock
no hickory
no dickory
no dock.

John Agard

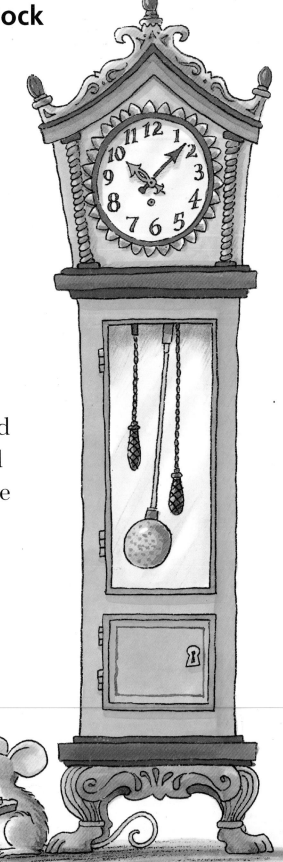